Journey Along a River

The Rhine

Jen Green

WAYLAND

This book is a differentiated text version of *A River Journey The Rhine* by Ronan Foley

This edition published in 2013 by Wayland
Copyright © 2013 Wayland

Wayland
338 Euston Road
London NW1 3BH

Wayland
Level 17/207 Kent Street
Sydney NSW 2000

Editor: Victoria Brooker
Designer: Stephen Prosser

Brtish Cataloguing in Publication Data
Green, Jen.
    The Rhine. -- (Journey along a river)
    1. Rhine River--Juvenile literature. 2. Rhine River Valley--
Juvenile literature.
    I. Title II. Series
    914.3'4-dc22

ISBN: 978 0 7502 7183 7

10 9 8 7 6 5 4 3 2 1

Printed in China

Wayland is a division of Hachette Children's Books,
an Hachette UK company.
www.hachette.co.uk

The website addresses (URLs) included in this book were valid at the time of going to press. However, because of the nature of the Internet, it is possible that some addresses may have changed, or sites may have changed or closed down since publication. While the author and Publisher regret any inconvenience this may cause readers,
no responsibility for any such changes can be accepted by either the author or the Publisher.

The maps in this book use a conical projection, and so the indicator for North on the main map is only approximate.

Picture Acknowledgements
Cover and 15: Bryan Pickering/Eye Ubiquitous title page: Eye Ubiquitous; 3 Hodder Wayland Picture Library; 5 Skyscan; 6 Hugh Rooney/Eye Ubiquitous; 7 (left) David Cumming/Eye Ubiquitous (right) Richard Wagner/AKG Photo; 8 Bernd Ducke/Britstock-Ifa; 9 Eye Ubiquitous; 10 Skyscan; 11 (left) Topham, (right) Neil Egerton/Travel Ink, (bottom) Ray Roberts/Impact; 12 Skyscan; 13 James Davis; 14 Topham; 16 Peter Siegenthaler/Britstock-Ifa; 17 Skyscan; 18 (left & right) Skyscan, 19 (left) Christophe Bluntzer/Impact, (right) James Davis; 19 (bottom) Jim McDonald/Corbis; 20 Popperfoto/Reuters; 21 (left) Skyscan, (right) Gerard Lacounette/Bios; 22 (left) Skyscan 4870, 22/23 (top) Gerard Lacounette/Bios; 23 Skyscan; 24 Stephen Coyne/Ecoscene; 24/25 James Davis; 26 Denis Bringard/Bios; 27 Bernd Ducke/Britstock-Ifa; 27 (bottom) Nick Weiseman/Eye Ubiquitous/Corbis; 28 Sally Morgan/Ecoscene; 29 David Cumming/Eye Ubiquitous; 30 Topham; 31 Bryan Pickering/Eye Ubiquitous, (top right) G. Graefenhain/Britstock-Ifa; 32 Robert Harding; 33 Popperfoto/Reuters; 34 Sally Morgan/Ecoscene; 35 Hodder Wayland Picture Library; 36 (top) Schmidbauer/Britstock-Ifa, (bottom) Skyscan; 37 Skyscan, (bottom right) Hodder Wayland Picture Library; 38 Robert Harding; 39 Geospace/Science Photo Library; 40 (left) Graham Kitching/Ecoscene; 40/41 Peter Palmer/Eye Ubiquitous; 41 (right) Larry Lee Photography/Corbis; 42 Mark Edwards/Still Pictures; 43 Robert Harding; 44 Mark Edwards/Still Pictures; 45 Anthony Cooper/Ecoscene

Contents

Words in **bold** can
be found in the
glossary on page 47.

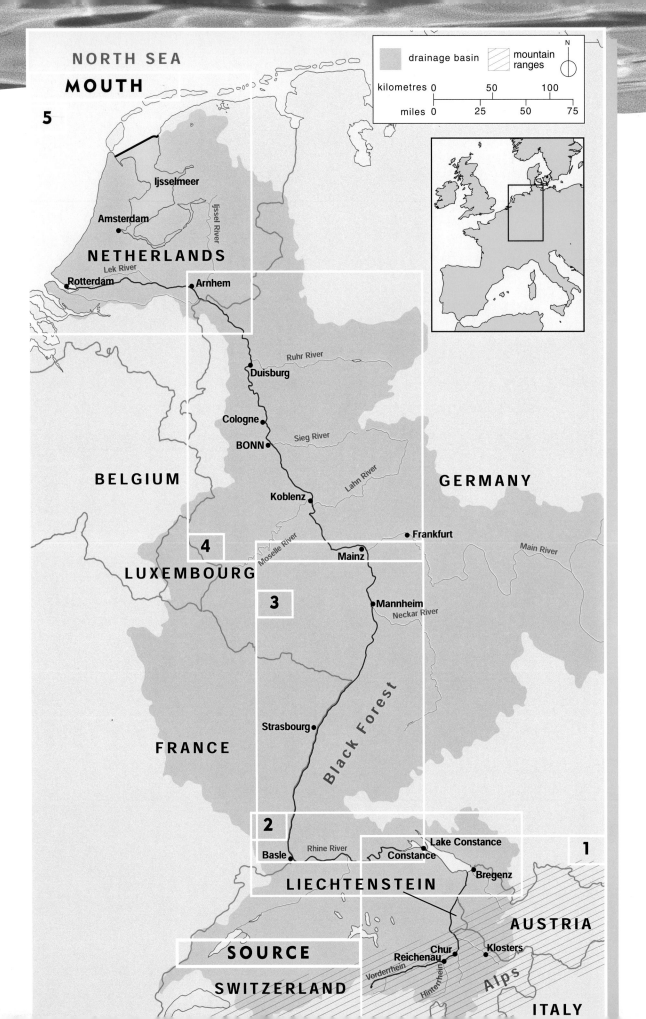

NORTH SEA

MOUTH

5

Ijsselmeer

Amsterdam

Ijssel River

NETHERLANDS

Lek River

Rotterdam   Arnhem

Ruhr River

Duisburg

Cologne

Sieg River

BONN

BELGIUM   GERMANY

Lahn River

Koblenz

Frankfurt

Moselle River   Main River

Mainz

4

LUXEMBOURG

3   Mannheim

Neckar River

Strasbourg

Black Forest

FRANCE

2

Rhine River   Lake Constance

Basle   Constance

Bregenz

LIECHTENSTEIN

AUSTRIA

SOURCE

Chur   Klosters

Reichenau

SWITZERLAND   Vorderrhein   Hinterrhein   Alps

ITALY

drainage basin   mountain ranges

N

kilometres 0   50   100

miles 0   25   50   75

1

Your guide to the river

The Rhine is one of Europe's longest rivers, at 1,320 kilometres long. Its journey takes it through six countries: Switzerland, Liechtenstein, Austria, Germany, France and the Netherlands. It often forms the border between countries. The map on page 4 shows the whole length of the Rhine river. The white squares show how our journey along the river has been divided into six chapters.

Map references

Each chapter has a map that shows the part of the river we are visiting. The numbered boxes show where interesting places are found.

The journey ahead

The Rhine begins life as a small stream high in the Swiss Alps. It ends as a mighty river flowing into the North Sea. On the way it flows through steep-sided valleys and past vineyards and castles. It visits lakes, cities and great ports. The Rhine has been important to the region's economy for centuries. Boats can travel along it for 800 kilometres, all the way from the town of Basle in Switzerland to the sea. It is one of the busiest waterways in the world. We are tracing the course of the Rhine all the way from the mountains to the sea. We will see how the river affects the landscape, and also the lives of the people who live along it. It's an incredible journey, so let's make a start!

We begin by flying over the Swiss Alps where the Rhine begins.

1. In the Alps

▼ **The Rhine begins high in the snow-capped Alps.**

Our journey begins with a flight over the Swiss mountains where the Rhine begins. We follow the river's course as far as Lake Constance. At first, the young river thunders down steep mountainsides. Later the ground begins to level out, and it becomes calmer. It flows through the tiny country of Liechtenstein. Before Lake Constance, we will see the first examples of how people control the river.

▲ The Rhine begins as a stream trickling from Lake Tuma.

▲ This poster is for Wagner's opera. It shows a dwarf stealing gold from the river bed.

The river's source

The place where a river starts is called the **source**. Most people believe Lake Tuma, high in the Swiss Alps, is the Rhine's source. This lake lies in a bowl surrounded by high mountains. The stream that trickles from the lake is the Rhine. At this point it is called the 'Vorderrhein' which means 'Front Rhine'.

Other people believe that the source of the Rhine is another stream. This is called the 'Hinterrhein' meaning 'Back Rhine'. It is fed by ice from the Rheinwaldhorn **Glacier** MAP REF 1. Later the two young rivers join.

Rhine gold

Many legends are told about the Rhine. The most famous legend comes from Germany and is about gold. It tells of a rich hoard of gold hidden in the mountains and guarded by a mountain people.

The German composer Richard Wagner was inspired by this legend. He used it for an opera, which he wrote in 1869. Gold and other metals are indeed found in the Alps near the source of the Rhine. In past times, the gold was used to make coins.

▲ **The alpenhorn was invented in Switzerland. You need a lot of room to play it!**

A harsh world

The mountains we are flying over are covered with ice and snow for about six months of the year. Only hardy plants and animals can survive here. One hardy animal is the chamois, or mountain goat. In the past, the skin of this animal was used to make soft leather. Now the chamois is very rare so no one is allowed to hunt it.

When the weather warms up in spring, the snow melts. Alpine plants, such as edelweiss, appear. This white, woolly flower is the Swiss national flower. Farmers here rear herds of cows, goats and sheep. In summer, these animals graze the high pastures. They spend winter in the valleys below.

From our small plane we can see where the Vorderrhein and Hinterrhein meet at Reichenau, near the city of Chur. From this point on the river is simply called the Rhine.

Swiss languages

The Rhine flows on through Switzerland. This country is known for watches, cheese, chocolate – and also languages. Four languages are spoken here. Three of them, French, German and Italian, are also spoken in neighbouring countries. The fourth, Romansh, is spoken only here. It is a mixture of Latin and Old French. Romansh is only spoken by about 50,000 people living in the Upper Rhine Valley.

Liechtenstein

The Rhine forms the border between Liechtenstein and Switzerland. The capital of Liechtenstein, Vaduz, sits on the river bank, guarded by an impressive castle.

▼ **This castle stands above Vaduz, the capital of Liechtenstein.**

We fly over Liechtenstein. Now the landscape starts to flatten. This tiny country is only 160 square kilometres in size – ten times smaller than Greater London. It is one of the world's smallest countries. Only about 36,000 people live here.

Liechtenstein may be small, but it is quite wealthy. Banking is a major industry here. It employs about 15 per cent of the country's workers. The dental industry is also important. Liechtenstein produces more false teeth than any other country in the world!

Taming the Rhine

Beyond Liechtenstein the Rhine forms the border between Switzerland and Austria. Here people have started to tame the river. From our plane we can see that small **dams** called **barrages** have been built across the river to cope with the changing flow. Each spring, melted snow swells the Rhine. The raging water washes rocks and soil downstream. Metal nets on the barrages catch **debris**, which could cause damage lower down.

The landscape is now flatter. The Rhine slows, and begins to drop the rocks and boulders it is carrying. Flooding used to be a problem here. In spring, the Rhine would burst its banks and spill over the surrounding land. In the nineteenth century, the river's course was **altered**. The banks were raised on either side. The **channel** was made straighter in many places. These changes were made to prevent flooding. However, rivers are very powerful. If the Rhine ever surges over the raised banks, the damage could be worse.

▼ **The Rhine has been forced to flow through a straight channel here. Rocks reinforce the banks.**

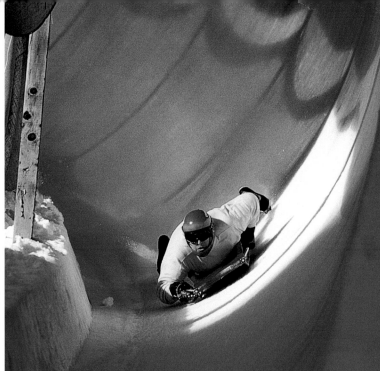

▲ **This famous bobsleigh run is called the Cresta Run.**

◄ **The ski resort of Davos in winter.**

Mountain jobs

Jobs in the mountains are changing. In past times, most people earned a living as farmers or hunters. Now, many people work in jobs connected with tourism.

Tourism is now the main industry in mountainous parts of Switzerland. In summer, people come to hike and climb here. In winter, they come for skiing and snow-boarding. Skiing is the main activity for tourists. Ski **resorts**, such as Davos and Klosters, are world famous. There is a well-known bobsleigh run near the resort (tourist town) of St Moritz.

Many people who work in tourism do different jobs throughout the year. In winter, they work as ski instructors. In summer, they may act as mountain guides. In autumn, they have a rest, or prepare the resort for winter!

We land and make our way to Lake Constance. At the lake, we continue by steamer.

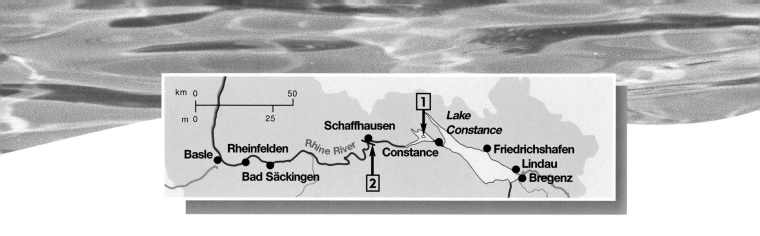

Map labels:
km 0 ... 50
m 0 ... 25
Schaffhausen
1
Lake Constance
Basle   Rheinfelden   Rhine River   Constance   Friedrichshafen
Bad Säckingen   Lindau
2   Bregenz

2. The Upper Rhine

Our steamer carries us along Lake Constance. Then we take a smaller boat to the spectacular Rhine Falls. Beyond the falls, boats can travel all the way to the sea. We travel west along the border between Switzerland and Germany. Around Rheinfelden river traffic increases, and the Rhine is also used to **generate** electricity.

▼ **The muddy Rhine enters the blue waters of Lake Constance.**

► **The walled town of Lindau is popular with tourists.**

Entering the lake

The Rhine enters Lake Constance near the town of Bregenz. From the air, we saw the muddy waters of the river entering the lake in a long stream, like a canal. The **sediment**-filled water drops to the bottom of the lake. It is like a waterfall, but underwater. This causes **turbulence**, and sometimes waves on the surface. After flowing the length of the lake for 65 kilometres, the Rhine emerges at the far end and continues west.

Lake Constance

Lake Constance is bordered by Germany, Switzerland and Austria. In German it is called Bodensee. It is surrounded by rolling hills and pretty towns. It is a popular place for tourists to visit. Over 170,000 tourists visit the city of Constance every year. This city is unusual. It stretches across the border between Germany and Switzerland, so it lies in two countries.

Tourists on the lake

Many tourists take a boat trip on the lake as we are doing. They enjoy the beautiful scenery and clean mountain air. People visit beautiful local towns, such as the walled town of Lindau. This stands on an island connected to the mainland by a **causeway**.

Our steamer calls at Reichenau Island MAP REF 1 where we visit St George's Church. This church is famous for its **frescoes,** which were painted in the ninth century.

Zeppelins

The town of Friedrichshafen lies on Lake Constance. It is famous as the home of airships called zeppelins. These were invented by a German nobleman, Ferdinand Graf von Zeppelin. The first zeppelin flew over Lake Constance in 1900. A total of 119 airships were built between 1900 and 1938.

During World War I, Germany used airships to drop bombs on Britain. After the war they were mainly used for luxury air travel. The cabin carrying passengers hung beneath a giant balloon, which was as long as two football pitches. In 1929, an airship called the 'Graf Zeppelin' took off from Lake Constance and flew all around the world.

In 1937, a zeppelin called the 'Hindenberg' caught fire as it came in to land in the USA. It exploded into flames because hydrogen gas inside the balloon and the silver paint on the airship were both highly **flammable**. A third of the people on board died. After the disaster airships stopped being made. However, a new-technology airship was launched in 2000 to celebrate a hundred years of zeppelins.

▼ **The first zeppelin made its first flight over Lake Constance in 1900.**

The Rhine Falls

About 20 kilometres beyond Lake Constance we reach another obstacle, the Rhine Falls MAP REF 2. This dramatic waterfall lies at Schaffhausen. The river races through a narrow **gorge** 150 metres wide. Then it plunges over a waterfall 23 metres high.

A waterfall forms where a river flows from a band of hard rocks onto softer rocks. The soft rocks wear away more quickly. This creates a shelf over which the water tumbles. The thundering water wears a deep pool at the bottom.

▲ **You get a great view of the Rhine Falls from the viewing station on the right of the photograph.**

The Rhine Falls formed about 15,000 years ago. They are most spectacular in spring, when **meltwater** from the mountains swells the river. Up to 1,080 cubic metres of water hurtles over the falls every second. That is enough to fill twenty Olympic-sized swimming pools every minute!

The Rhine Falls are a popular tourist attraction. About 1.5 million people come to see the falls every year.

Busy river

The Rhine is Europe's busiest waterway. It carries more traffic than any other river in the world. About 200 million tonnes of cargo pass along the river each year. That is about four times as much cargo as travels along the Danube, in Central Europe.

The Rhine is not fully **navigable** until the town of Rheinfelden, about 50 kilometres below the Rhine Falls. Between the Rhine Falls and Rheinfelden the river is blocked by a series of dams. Planners originally hoped that boats would be able to travel upriver as far as Lake Constance. But the upper Rhine proved too dangerous.

The Rhine is now part of a network of European waterways. A **canal** near Nürnberg links it to the Danube. The Rhine-Main-Danube Canal is an important trade route as it links the Atlantic Ocean and the Black Sea.

▲ **A speedboat carries tourists down the Rhine.**

Water to energy

In the late nineteenth century, European scientists were experimenting with methods of producing electricity. They realised that fast-flowing water could provide a constant and free source of power. Flowing water could be used to turn **generators** to produce electricity. Electricity made in this way is called **hydroelectric** power, or HEP for short.

Europe's first HEP station was built at Rheinfelden in 1898. Other HEP plants were later built on minor rivers called **tributaries**, that tumble down from the mountains to join the Rhine. These tributaries are ideal for generating electricity because the steep ground makes the water fast-flowing.

Damming the river

When a hydroelectric plant is planned, a dam is usually built across the river. This controls the speed and power of the flow. Water builds up behind the dam to form an **artificial** lake called a **reservoir**. The dam and lake are useful in other ways, too. The reservoir stores water and the dam helps to prevent flooding, by controlling the flow of water and releasing it gradually.

HEP stations produce energy without burning coal or gas. Coal- and gas-burning power stations produce a lot of air **pollution**. HEP plants don't pollute the air, so they are kinder to the **environment.**

▼ **The hydroelectric station at Rheinfelden (bottom left in the photograph) is over a hundred years old.**

Historic towns

As we continue west along the Rhine, we pass a number of historic towns. At Rheinau an abbey stands on a small **peninsula** which juts out into the river. The abbey was built around 1700.

Later, we pass under an old bridge in the town of Bad Säckingen. This covered bridge was one of the first bridges to be built across the Rhine. It took fifty years to build, between 1570 and 1620. The bridge spans 200 metres across the river. A white line in the middle marks the border between Germany and Switzerland.

As we approach Basle, we pass the town of Kaiseraugst. In 1982, Roman treasure was discovered at an old Roman town nearby. This town was

▲ **Germany, France and Switzerland meet at this point on the river.**

◄ **The old bridge at Bad Säckingen.**

abandoned, but a smaller Roman settlement which was called Basilea survives. It is now the city of Basle.

The Swiss city of Basle marks a turning point for the Rhine. Here the river suddenly heads north. A tall post in the river marks the border between France, Germany and Switzerland.

We leave the boat to explore the city of Basle. This beautiful city feels quite different to other towns we have passed through. Many people here speak a local **dialect** of German, mixed with a bit of French!

▲ The Rhine is quite wide at Basle. Large boats can use the river here.

◀ Fassnacht celebrations in Basle.

Carnival in Basle

Basle is famous for its carnival, which is called 'Fassnacht'. This carnival is held just before Lent – the period of fasting before Easter. People traditionally celebrated before the fast began. This tradition is 2,000 years old. Carnivals are held in many European towns, especially in Germany.

Basle Fassnacht is famous for its street parades. People wear colourful costumes and march through the streets. Bands play music and lanterns light up the route.

At Basle, we catch a ride on a barge for the next stage of our journey.

Mainz

Worms
Ludwigshafen Mannheim
Heidelberg

GERMANY

Speyer

Main River

Neckar River

Karlsruhe
Baden-Baden

FRANCE

Strasbourg

Black Forest

Vosges Mountains

Rhine River

km 0   50
m 0   25

1 Basle
Rheinfelden

3. The working Rhine

Beyond Basle we reach a section of the Rhine that has been changed a lot. The channel has been straightened and also raised above the countryside. We follow the river north past the historic towns of Strasbourg and Mainz. This part of the river is used for industry as well as transport. However, industry can cause problems, such as pollution.

▼ **This modern building is the home of the European Parliament.**

FRANCE 100 m

FERMETURE POSSIBLE SANS PREAVIS POUR RAISONS DE SECURITE SCHLIESSUNG AUS SICHERHEITSGRÜNDEN OHNE HINWEIS MÖGLICH

▲ The Rhine is now up to 100 metres wide. France lies on the left, Germany on the right in this photograph.

◄ A border crossing displays the EU flag. The sign warns that the gate will be closed in an emergency.

Marking the border

Rivers often form the borders between countries, and the Rhine is no exception. Here, it forms the boundary between Germany and France.

In the past, the boundaries of France and Germany were not along the river. For example, the French region west of the Rhine, Alsace-Lorraine, was part of Germany between 1870 and 1919.

European headquarters

In 1979, the city of Strasbourg became the home of the European Parliament – the governing body of the European Union (EU). This decision reflected the strong links between two of the Union's members, Germany and France. We explore the city and the parliament buildings.

The Euro

In 1999, France, Germany and nine other EU members stopped using their old currencies and **adopted** one currency – the Euro. By 2012, six other European countries had also adopted the Euro.

Barge traffic

The Rhine and its tributaries flow though one of western Europe's main industrial areas. The river is used to transport bulky cargoes, such as coal, grain, timber, oil, chemicals and iron ore. These goods are carried by barges, such as the one we are using. The barges can be up to 100 metres long – the length of a football pitch.

Transporting goods by barge is cheaper than going by road or rail. Barges also use relatively little fuel, which is good for the environment. But they are slow. Journeys have to be planned carefully to make sure that goods arrive on time.

The changing river

The channel of a river changes naturally over time. Bends gradually become deep loops called **meanders**. This happens as the river wears away the soil on the outside of the bends, where the **current** is fast and powerful. The bed of the river may also become more shallow as sediment builds up.

▲ **Barges are long and narrow, so they can pass one another easily.**

Rhine ship canal

North of Basle, engineers have changed the channel of the river to make it easier for boats to use. The Rhine has been straightened and also deepened to allow large ships to pass along the river.

A new channel has been built between raised banks. This now sits a few metres above the surrounding land. The old route of the Rhine, called the 'ResteRhein', lies to the east and below us MAP REF 1 . The new channel carries most of the river's water. The old channel has become a quiet backwater. It takes the overflow after heavy rain.

Locks

The ship canal we are using has **locks** which lower or raise the water level. This allows us to pass along the river. The locks help to make sure the channel always has enough water to keep larger boats afloat. There are twelve large locks between Rheinfelden and Baden-Baden, 170 kilometres downstream.

◀ Ships bypass the dam on the right of the photograph using the lock on the left. The old curving river channel lies to the left of the straight canal.

▼ The old river channel provides a home for plants and animals.

▲ **Nuclear power stations are a familiar sight on the west bank of the Rhine in France.**

Nuclear power

Nuclear power stations are a common sight along this stretch of the Rhine, particularly on the French side. These power plants need large amounts of water for cooling, so rivers make good places for them.

France has a lot of nuclear power stations. In 2012, over 75 per cent of France's electricity came from nuclear power – more than any other European country.

Germany also has nuclear plants. Until 2011, it got one quarter of its electricity from nuclear power. However, German nuclear plants are gradually being closed down. People became worried about the dangers of radiation after an accident at a nuclear plant in Russia in 1986.

The Black Forest

Germany's Black Forest lies to the east of the river. This is one of the most beautiful and popular areas in Germany. It covers a large area of rolling hills. Much of the Black Forest is covered with dark conifer trees. These forests are criss-crossed with 23,000 kilometres of trails for walkers and cyclists.

The authorities here are very keen on protecting the environment. There are

very strict planning controls on all new developments. We spot a tall spire on the horizon. It is the spire of the cathedral at Freiburg-im-Breisgau, the capital of the Black Forest region.

Clocks and cakes

Farming is important to this region. The mild climate allows farmers to grow grain, potatoes, garden plants, hops and tobacco. Clock-making is an unusual local industry. You can even do a tour of the region's most amazing clocks, which is called the Route of Clocks.

The Black Forest is famous for black forest gateau, a delicious cake made with chocolate, cream and cherries. Try some, but avoid eating too much, as this cake is very rich!

▼ **The rolling hills of the Black Forest lie east of the Rhine.**

Polluted river

Like many rivers, the Rhine has a long history of pollution. For hundreds of years, sewage from towns and villages entered the water. Since the early nineteenth century, waste from industries, such as chemical factories, has been dumped in the Rhine.

By the mid-twentieth century, the river was so poisonous that local fish, such as salmon, had died out. The building of canals, locks and **weirs** also disturbed the natural habitat.

River pollution is a sensitive issue where a river flows through more than one country. Countries downstream are polluted if an accident happens higher up. In 1986, the Rhine was seriously polluted after an accident at a chemical factory near Basle. Thirty tonnes of poisonous chemicals entered the river. All river life died for 100 kilometres downstream.

Cleaning up

In 1987, after the accident, the six countries that share the Rhine launched a campaign to clear up the river. Strict laws now control the amount of waste that can be dumped here. Companies that break the rules are traced and fined.

A pumping station near Basle checks the water quality every six minutes, 24 hours a day. Salmon are now found in the river again – a sure sign that things are improving.

▼ **Salmon swimming upstream use the steps on the left to pass the barrier on the right.**

Cathedral bells

As we continue our journey into Germany we pass many historic towns. Cities such as Worms, Speyer and Mainz are known for their cathedrals. Church bells ring out as we pass through.

Worms Cathedral is the oldest. It was built around AD 1000. This cathedral was

▲ **Heidelberg is a beautiful German town with many old buildings. It lies on a tributary of the Rhine.**

made famous by Martin Luther, who founded the Protestant faith. Luther founded this new faith in 1517 after going to a religious meeting in Worms. These meetings were called diets, so this one was called the Diet of Worms!

We leave our barge at Mainz. We board a hydrofoil to carry us down the Rhine.

4. The Lower Rhine

The next part of our journey takes us through classic Rhine country. This stretch of the river has steep-sided valleys, vineyards and historic towns. Later, we approach the Ruhr, an industrial region. Several large rivers join the Rhine, adding their water. This can make the river dangerous – it's a good thing our captain knows these waters well!

▼ **Rhine country – a steep-sided valley with pretty towns along the banks of the river.**

▲ Vineyards line the steep slopes above the Rhine.

Rhine Gorge

As we leave Mainz, the river heads west, and then north again. Soon we enter the Rhine Gorge MAP REF 1. This gorge has formed where the river reaches an area of hard volcanic rocks. The water found a line of weakness in the rocks and flowed along it. Over time it has worn a deep groove in the landscape.

The Rhine Gorge is very narrow. In fact, the channel is only about as wide as the river that runs through it! This is because the river has cut down through the rock faster than rain, ice and frost have worn away the sides.

Vineyards

Wine-growing is an important industry here. The hillsides are lined with vineyards. The sunny, south-facing slopes and well-drained soil are ideal for growing vines.

Germany is among the top ten wine-producing nations in the world. This region is the most important wine-growing area in Germany. But two-thirds of the vineyards here are small – less than 30 hectares.

Most of the wines produced here are white. This is because white grapes grow best in the relatively cold climate. Most of the wine that is sold abroad is of only medium quality. The Germans keep the best wines for themselves!

The tourist trail

Our hydrofoil is fast. It can skim along at up to 65 kilometres per hour. At that speed you can cover the 300 kilometres between Mainz and Cologne and back again in half a day. This fast transport link has opened this stretch of the river for tourism. Several companies run tours along the gorge. Tourists stop off to visit a castle or vineyard on the way.

Tourism has been important here for centuries. The first tourist steamships began operating in the 1820s. The largest side-wheeled paddle steamer in the world still carries tourists along this stretch of the river.

▶ **The Lorelei Rock overlooks a dangerous stretch of the Rhine.**

▼ **This paddle steamer, the 'Goethe', has carried tourists since 1826.**

Legend of the Lorelei

We now enter one of the famous parts of the Rhine – the Lorelei Valley. We pass romantic ruined castles on the banks. At St Goarshausen we reach Lorelei Rock MAP REF 2 . This is one of the region's top attractions. It is also one of the most dangerous stretches of the river, with shifting currents and hidden **shoals**.

The Lorelei Rock is 133 metres high. A legend says it was the home of a beautiful woman called the Lorelei. She lured sailors to their death in the waters below. The 'Song of the Lorelei' is a famous German song.

The Rhine in Flames

In August, the spectacular Rhine in Flames festival takes place. Towns along the river 'burn' as a group of 80 boats sail past. Buildings along the banks place red lights in their windows and on terraces to create the effect of burning. Giant flares are set off near castles and churches. The red glow and smoke make the 'fires' look real. Around 30,000 people watch from the boats. Another 500,000 sight-seers line the river banks.

▶ **The Rhine in Flames festival is held each summer.**

Rhine tributaries

We are cruising down the Rhine between the cities of Boppard and Bonn. As we head downstream from Boppard we notice more tributaries joining the Rhine. These have been a feature all along the river's journey. The River Main joined the Rhine at Mainz after flowing 525 kilometres from eastern Germany. At Koblenz the Moselle joins, having flowed from the Vosges Mountains in France, to the southwest. The Lahn and the Sieg also join from the east.

▲ **The Moselle River joins the Rhine at Deutsches Eck (German Corner). The Moselle is clear, the Rhine is murky.**

Flood danger

Many of these tributaries are carefully managed to control flooding. Dams and reservoirs help to regulate the amount of water that joins the Rhine. However, big rivers like the Rhine are still very powerful. When heavy rainfall swells the river, it can spill over its banks, causing flooding. Towns and farmland can be swamped.

▲ **The Rhine burst its banks in 1995, causing flooding in Cologne.**

Floods in Cologne

The city of Cologne is regularly hit by floods. In the 1990s, four serious floods struck here. The worst was in 1993, when the river rose over 10 metres above its normal level. Five people died and 10,000 litres of heating oil leaked into the river, causing pollution.

Portable flood barriers have been brought in to protect suburbs that are particularly at risk of flooding. These successfully prevented damage to homes during a later flood in 1999. But the river is still unpredictable.

More carnivals

The end of February is carnival time in the historic cathedral city of Cologne. The festival lasts for five days, which are called 'crazy days'. On one day women are allowed to play pranks on men, such as cutting off their ties!

The highlight of the festival is the last day. It is called 'Rosenmontag' which means 'Raging Monday'. There is a big procession. Giant figures, floats and horse-drawn carriages parade through the streets. Crowds cheer and over a hundred bands play music. These processions can stretch for over five kilometres and take three hours to pass.

◀ **Coal, plastic and other goods are loaded onto barges at the port of Duisburg.**

Inland ports

The Rhine is the most important waterway in western Europe. Over 100 million tonnes of cargo pass along this section of the river every year. Large barges carry iron ore, oil, petrol, coal and grain downstream. We also see tugs pushing up to six linked barges.

Most barges call at Duisport in Duisburg. This is one of the world's largest inland ports. Duisburg lies at the point where the River Ruhr joins the Rhine. The Ruhr District is one of the most important industrial areas in western Europe.

Duisport developed where small boats carrying coal along the Ruhr needed to transfer their cargo onto bigger boats. The large boats are cheaper to run but cannot sail up the Ruhr because it is too shallow. It takes us a long time to pass Duisport. It covers about 1,000 hectares – the size of nearly 2,000 football pitches!

Home of industry

The Ruhr District developed in the early nineteenth century during the Industrial Revolution. A number of towns along the Ruhr and the Rhine – Essen, Duisburg, Dortmund and Gelsenkirchen – developed around iron, coal and steel works. Eventually they merged to make one huge urban area. Iron, coal and steel production are still important here. We watch barges pass laden with cargo.

▲ This small tug can push six fully loaded barges in front of it.

Cleaner fuels

In recent years, this district has changed as minerals, such as coal, have become scarce. In any case, people now prefer 'cleaner' fuels, which cause less pollution. Coal and other traditional industries are becoming less important, and new industries, such as engineering and computing, are growing.

◄ **Great crested grebes live in local nature reserves.**

▼ **Sailing is popular on this part of the Rhine.**

Enjoying the river

Between Duisburg and the Dutch border we pass close to the towns of Kleve and Wesel. This area is known as the 'Unterer Niederrhein' or Under Lower Rhine. About forty per cent of it is nature reserve, which covers 25,000 hectares. The reserve is mostly wetland. This is a great place to go bird-watching. We look for lapwing, golden plovers, green-winged teal and great crested grebes.

The nature reserve includes several lakes that are old gravel pits as well as the open river, with sand and pebble shores. Here you can enjoy water sports such as sailing, wind-surfing, swimming, fishing and camping.

Farming and pollution

The flat plain around us is important for agriculture. Maize, tobacco, sugar beet and vegetables are among the crops grown here. Farmers use fertilizers on their fields to increase crop yields. The downside is that these chemicals cause

▲ **Fertilizers sprayed on fields can wash into the river.**

pollution. They build up in the soil and also drain into streams that empty into the Rhine.

The fertilizers used in farming can kill fish and river plants. This is because they encourage the growth of tiny water plants called algae. The algae grow rapidly until large mats of floating weed cover the water surface. Large mats of algae form on the water's surface. This prevents sunlight from reaching the levels below.

The water becomes starved of oxygen, which can kill fish and other river life.

Preventing pollution

Nowadays strict laws prevent farms and factories along the banks of the Rhine from polluting the river. However, streams can carry chemicals used on the surrounding plain into the river. This means some fertilizer still gets into the Rhine. The only way to prevent it would be to ban the use of chemicals in all farms in the region. Chemical free farming is called organic farming.

We board an ocean-going cargo ship at Emmerich. We head towards the Rhine delta.

5. The Rhine delta

As the Rhine approaches the sea its course becomes complicated. It splits into many channels as it crosses a vast low-lying **delta**. As we weave between canals and windmills, it becomes hard to work out exactly where we are! We decide to stick to the main channel. This flows past Rotterdam before we reach our journey's end – the North Sea.

The map shows:

NORTH SEA

Afsluitdijk

km 0 — 50
m 0 — 25

Ijsselmeer

Amsterdam

NETHERLANDS

Ijssel River

Crooked Rhine River

Utrecht

Rotterdam

Lek River

Arnhem

Waal River

▼ The Rhine splits into many channels in the Netherlands. The channels are linked by canals.

Bridges and battles

We pass under a historic bridge at Arnhem. Bridges such as this one were of military importance during World War II. The Allies (Britain and the USA) fought the German army to gain control of the bridges in 1944, when Germany was retreating from France.

As the Germans retreated, they blew up bridges after crossing them to slow down the Allies. The Allies raced to capture the bridges before they were blown up. These battles have been made into films such as 'Saving Private Ryan' and 'A Bridge Too Far'.

Many channels

The Rhine slows down as it approaches the sea. As it slows it drops the sediment it is carrying. Over thousands of years, sediment dropped by the river has formed a vast, swampy delta. The river splits into three main channels as it makes its way through the delta. The Lek flows west past Rotterdam, and enters the sea at the Hook of Holland. To the south, the Waal River drains into an arm of the North Sea. The third channel, called the Crooked Rhine, passes the city of Utrecht and then continues west to the sea. The delta is a vast lowland area. It stretches from north of Amsterdam southwards as far as Antwerp in Belgium. We follow the Lek, which many people believe is the main route through this swampy region.

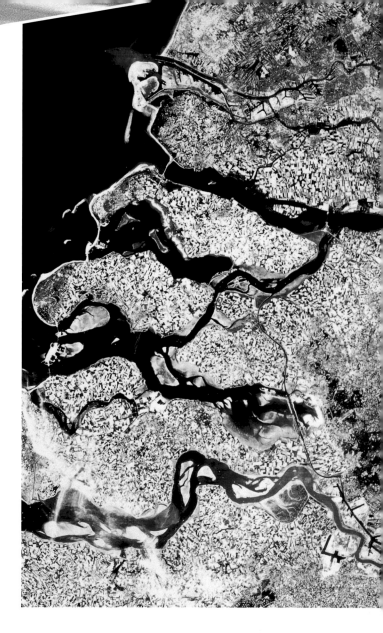

▲ **This photo taken by a satellite shows some of the many channels of the delta. The Lek is the most northerly channel shown here.**

Flood prevention

Much of the Netherlands is very low-lying. Nearly a quarter of the whole country is below sea level. This creates a serious risk of flooding, both from rivers and the sea. The Rhine delta includes a lot of land that has been reclaimed from the sea. High walls called dykes have been built to keep the sea out. They also prevent the land behind the wall from getting salty.

Since the 1990s, water levels in the Rhine and other local rivers have been very high due to heavy rainfall. In 1995, rivers rose so high they spilled over the dykes onto the surrounding land. Farms and several towns were flooded.

To avoid this problem, some dykes are being moved back. In some cases farmland is being allowed to return to marsh. This will allow local rivers to flow more freely. **Water meadows** will soak up extra water, making flooding less likely.

◄ **Dykes along the coast keep out the sea. An inlet of the North Sea called the Zuider Zee is shown on the right here.**

▼ **Tulip-growing is an important industry in the Rhine Delta.**

Tulip trade

Farming, especially flower-growing, is important here. The Netherlands produces about nine billion flower bulbs each year! Tulips are the most famous flower. The country produces about 80 per cent of the world's tulips. Tulip fields cover over 8,500 hectares of land.

Dutch land and people

The Netherlands is one of the most densely populated countries in Europe. In 2009, there were 16.7 million people living in a country of just 41,526 square kilometres. That gives an average of 477 people for each square kilometre. This compares to 257 people per square kilometre in Britain and 33 people per square kilometre in the United States. It's no wonder land is precious here. The Dutch have been reclaiming land from the sea for 400 years. One of the biggest schemes took place in the 1930s. A dam was built across a large, shallow inlet of the sea called the Zuider Zee. The area behind was drained to make new land, which the Dutch call **polders** MAP REF 1 . Around 165,000 hectares of land were created for new farms and towns.

▼ **Amsterdam, the Dutch capital, is a crowded city.**

Wind power

The Netherlands is famous for its windmills. They have played an important part in the country's development. From the seventeenth century, windmills have been used to drain low-lying land.

Scoops turned by the wind collected water from the marshy land. The water was tipped back into streams and rivers. By the mid-nineteenth century more than 10,000 windmills dotted the Dutch landscape. Gradually electric pumps replaced them, and now only about a thousand remain.

Now modern wind **turbines** are being used to generate energy. This new technology makes the most of the flat, windy landscape. A single hundred-metre wind turbine can provide enough power for 800 families.

▲ **The windmill on the left and wind turbines on the right both use wind energy.**

By 2009, the Netherlands was a leading wind producer. Wind energy provides a smaller percentage of the country's electricity than in Denmark, Spain, Portugal and Germany. But Dutch wind technology is growing fast. There are already several offshore wind farms – including two close to the mouth of the Rhine.

Rotterdam and Europoort

The Lek has been widened near the mouth so large ocean-going ships can use it. We follow this channel to Rotterdam, one of the world's largest ports.

Rotterdam handles traffic for three of Europe's biggest economies: the Netherlands, France and Germany. In 2007, over 400 million tonnes of cargo passed through the port. In 1957, the Dutch decided to build an extra port, called Europoort MAP REF 2 . This is located right on the North Sea, mostly on land that has been reclaimed. The docks of Rotterdam and Europoort cover 105 square kilometres and stretch for 40 kilometres along the river.

Europoort makes use of the latest technology and equipment. We pass the 'disaster area' where fire and other emergency services practise dealing with large-scale accidents. For example, a tanker is deliberately set on fire so fire fighters can practise putting it out.

▼ **Ships of all shapes and sizes can dock at Rotterdam, Europe's biggest port.**

Silting up the delta

The Rhine flows very slowly in the delta. Slow-flowing water has less energy to carry sediment, so the river drops huge amounts of **silt** here. This makes the channel shallow. The river has to be **dredged** regularly to keep it deep enough for ships to use.

The port of Rotterdam alone has to remove about ten million tonnes of silt from the harbour each year. The sediment gets dumped out to sea.

The sediment contains **pollutants**, such as oil and chemicals, released by factories upriver. In the 1980s, scientists believed that the river was responsible for about 40 per cent of all the pollution in the North Sea.

Cleaning up

In recent years, the authorities have been trying to clean up pollution in the delta. One method is to clean the sediment itself, but this is very expensive. It is cheaper to reduce the amount of pollution that enters the river. Nowadays, the river is a lot cleaner than it was, but there is still room for improvement.

◄ **Pollution from the delta enters the North Sea.**

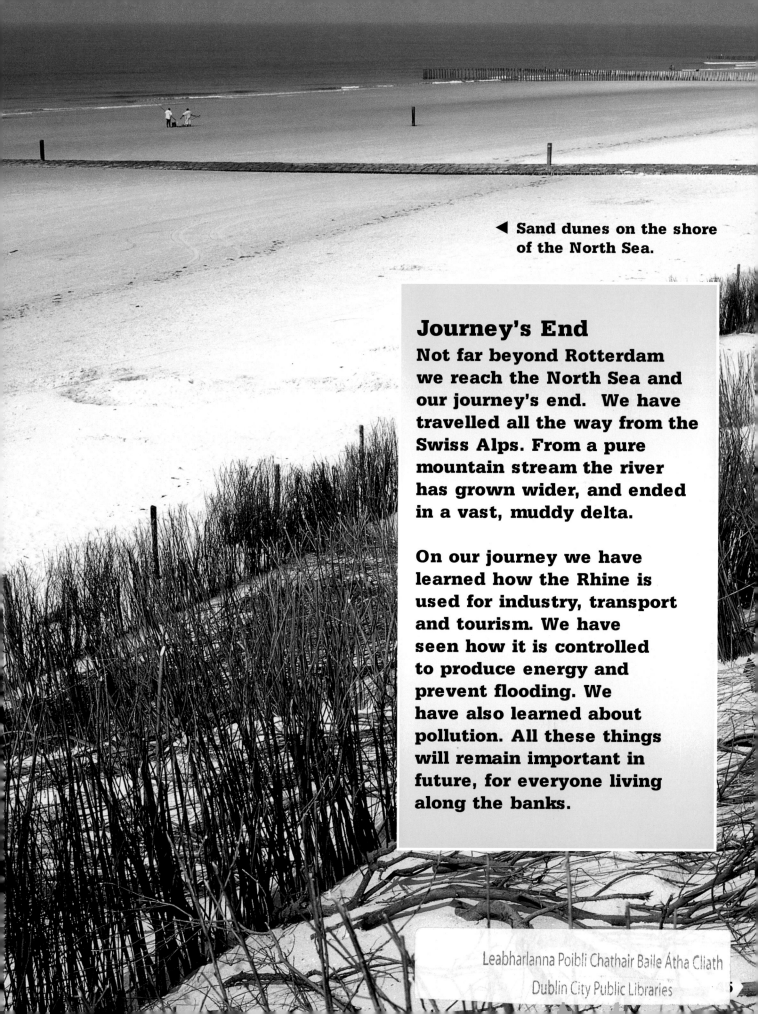

◄ **Sand dunes on the shore of the North Sea.**

Journey's End

Not far beyond Rotterdam we reach the North Sea and our journey's end. We have travelled all the way from the Swiss Alps. From a pure mountain stream the river has grown wider, and ended in a vast, muddy delta.

On our journey we have learned how the Rhine is used for industry, transport and tourism. We have seen how it is controlled to produce energy and prevent flooding. We have also learned about pollution. All these things will remain important in future, for everyone living along the banks.

The Rhine falls over 1,800 metres on its 1,320-kilometre journey from the Alps to the North Sea.

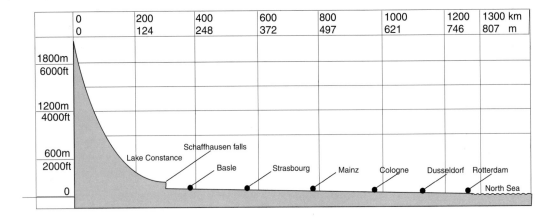

	0	200	400	600	800	1000	1200	1300 km
	0	124	248	372	497	621	746	807 m

1800m / 6000ft

1200m / 4000ft

600m / 2000ft

0

Lake Constance

Schaffhausen falls

Basle

Strasbourg

Mainz

Cologne

Dusseldorf

Rotterdam

North Sea

Further information

Websites

A webpage on the Rhine from Factmonster, an online information centre for young users. Use the search function to find more information about rivers: http://www.factmonster.com/ce6/world/A0841717.html

Facts about the River Rhine: http://www.woodlands-junior.kent.sch.uk/Homework/rivers/rhine.htm

A picture gallery of the Rhine in Germany and Austria: http://www.lehigh.edu/~brb0/GermanyAustria/rhine.html

Find out about how pollution along the Rhine has been cleaned up, and see a map of the river: http://www.unesco.org/courier/2000_06/uk/planet.htm

Books

Country Topics: Germany by Ting Morris, Rachel Wright (Watts, 2007)

Discover Countries: Germany by Camilla de la Bédoyère (Wayland, 2009)

Geography Detective: Rivers by Jen Green (Wayland, 2006)

Geography Now: Rivers around the World by Jen Green (Wayland, 2008)

Glossary

adopt to take on or use.

alter to change.

artificial something that has been made by people.

barrage a dam.

bypass to go past something.

canal an artificial waterway.

causeway a raised path over water or a marsh.

channel the passage through which a river flows, or to direct water a certain way.

current a regular flow of water in a certain direction.

dam a barrier that diverts or holds back water.

debris loose pieces of rock.

delta a flat, swampy area that forms as a river drops sediment at its mouth.

dialect a form of a language spoken in a particular area.

dredge to deepen a river so that ships can use it.

environment the surroundings in which plants, animals and people live.

flammable of something that burns easily.

fresco a wall painting.

generate to produce something, such as electricity.

generator a machine used to produce electricity.

glacier a mass of ice that flows slowly downhill.

gorge a deep, narrow valley with sheer sides.

hydroelectricity electricity that is made using fast-flowing water.

lock an enclosed section of a river where the water level can be lowered or raised.

meander a looping bend on a river.

meltwater water produced by melting snow and ice.

navigable of a waterway that can be used by ships and boats.

peninsula a piece of land that juts out into water.

polder an area of land that has been drained and reclaimed from the sea.

pollutant a substance that causes pollution.

pollution when the air, water or soil is harmed by a substance that doesn't belong there.

portable of something that can be carried.

reservoir an artificial lake used to store water, made by damming a river or stream.

resort a town or village which receives many visitors and where tourism is important.

sediment soil or small stones carried along by a river.

shoal an underwater sandbank.

silt fine sand or mud carried along by a river.

source the place where a river begins.

tributary a minor river or stream that joins the main river.

turbine a machine powered by steam or water that is used to produce electricity.

turbulence when water or air is disturbed by swirling currents.

water meadow a wet grassy area by a stream or river.

weir a small dam on a river built to control the flow.

Index